Blended Reality

Poems and Thoughts for Stepmoms, Blended Families, and the People that Support Us.

Poems and Illustrations by
Michaele-Lynne Jacot

Copyright© 2015 by Michaele-Lynne Jacot
Blended Reality: Poems and Thoughts for Stepmoms, Blended Families, and the People that Support Us.

ISBN-13: 978-0692534489 (Michaele-Lynne Jacot)

ISBN-10: 0692534482

All rights reserved. No part of this book may be reproduced or transmitted in any form or by and means, electronic or mechanical, including photocopying, recording or by any information storage or retrieval system, without written permission from the author, except for the inclusion of brief quotations in a review.

Copyright© 2016 by Michaele-Lynne Jacot: First Edition, 2015
Published in the United States of America

About this book:

Michaele-Lynne Jacot had never given a thought to writing a book, however, she had been inspired to write and journal more now that she was part of a blended family. The poems came together quickly, and she soon decided to attend a book publishing class. Miss Jacot hopes to touch stepmoms and other women all over the country (and maybe the world!), who experience the day to day happenings of blended family life. Perhaps it will also catch the eyes of someone like Ellen (who would be great for publicity!)! The poems are in print as they were written chronologically and it is quite possible there will be more books in the future! It is truly hoped that these poems bring you joy, comfort, and a sense of knowing that you are not alone on this journey!

This book is dedicated to each and every person who has been affected by the realities of blended family life (for better or for worse!); Most notably, my partner through it all — Josh.

...and a very special shout out and "Thanks!" to Orla, Colleen, Heather, Mary & Katie.

A Note to My Step-Daughters:

You may not understand why I write as I do, or where I am coming from. You must know the length of time I took to debate publishing my thoughts for the world to see. It took me months to decide to pursue; the only thing holding me back was potential hurt or embarrassment that you might feel from my words. Please know that I have taken some liberty with a few of these poems (mostly for rhyming purposes!). Please know that I in no way intend to hurt you. Please know that I do this for my own therapy, and truly believe that others can benefit from my words as well. You may not understand, you may be mad, but I hope if you are that someday you will understand and forgive. I love you both more than you know.

Ways to be a Mother

There are many ways to be a mother,
Giving birth is only one.

There are many ways to be a mother,
Here's a little list for fun…

Cheering throughout nights and days,
At games, ceremonies, recitals, and plays.

Making lunches, brushing hair,
Helping with homework, and the science fair.

Waking up in the middle of the night,
To help sooth nightmares and other frights.

Putting on sunscreen, bug spray, and aloe,
Boots, mittens and hot chocolate with 'mallows.

There are many ways to be a mother,
Giving birth is only one.

There are many ways to be a mother,
Here's a little list for fun.

Boxes and Bags

Boxes and bags, totes and jars,
Fill up my basement, attic, and yard.
Crates and cases add to the clutter,
"Where does all of it come from?" I mutter…

Your things are precious, I understand,
But can't we organize our land?
Worksheets, paper and homework too,
Our kitchen table is quite a zoo!

All I ask for is a little cooperation,
In this task of household organization.
Though I'm the only one that seems to care,
If the floor appears to be clear and bare.

Should I give in or hold my ground?
Want to know what I've found?
Take a deep breath and grab some wine,
Don't worry away your valuable time.

Boxes and bags, totes and jars,
Fill up my basement, attic, and yard.
Now grab a glass, or 3 or 4…
Do what you can – nothing less, nothing more.

The Black Hole (aka Mom's House)

Where did that shirt go?
I think I know…

It traveled to Mom's house,
Long ago.

Will it ever be seen at Dads again?
Ha - you're dreaming! Really - are you serious?

You really think you're going to see that shirt again?

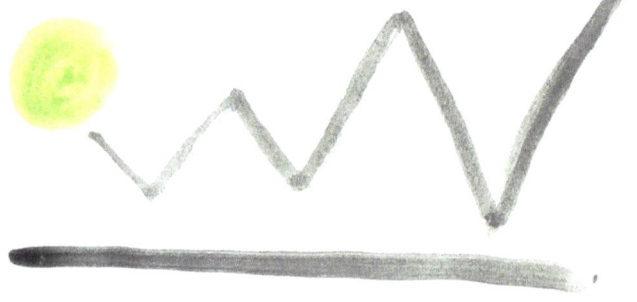

(Step) Mom Always Says, "Never Play Ball in the House!"

Soccer balls, basketballs, hacky-sacks.
Played inside? Imagine that.

I said no, he said yes.
I guess I'll go upstairs and rest.

Soccer balls, basketballs, hacky-sacks.
Bouncing off the walls and back.

He said yes, I said no.
Outside for a walk I'll go…

The Ex-in-laws

What do you make of your ex-in-laws?
Do they want to gobble you in their jaws?
Do they want to scratch you with their claws?
Do they pick out all your minor flaws?

Who gives a crap, I say to you!
They are over, done with, through!
Until you see them next week at school…
And soccer, ballet, the park and the pool.

What do you make of your ex-in-laws?
Do they want to gobble you in their jaws?
Do they want to scratch you with their claws?
Do they pick out all your minor flaws?

Who gives a crap, I say to you!
They are over, done with, through!
Just smile, nod, and hold your head up high
Or just get high…no, I'm just kidding. But really,
maybe just get high. It might help you to relax a bit.

*Please note that I do not support or condone the use of marijuana to escape your problems — but merely hope to bring a smile to your face.

Eating Healthy

Healthy meals I try to make,
With veggies, fruits, and sometimes steak.
But whine and moan you always do,
Until I make a cabbage stew?!

(Seriously, They loved that shit.)

Just as Hard

I suppose it's just as hard for you,
All this confusion I'm going through.
Yet decisions are always yours to make,
My thoughts and ideas you don't want to take.

I suppose it's just as hard for you,
To have another woman around, too.
Yet you make all the calls and shots,
Communicating with us not.

I suppose it's just as hard for you,
To try on the other person's shoe.
Yet I always try to be understanding,
While you immerse yourself with blaming.

I suppose it's just as hard for you,
To try to start things out anew.
But this I truly beg of you,
See things from our point of view.

Your Children

Each day I love them more you see,
They grow inside, but differently.
For they are a part of you,
And to my heart I must be true.

Our bond is stronger every day,
Because now, "I love you," we all say.
I see so much of them in you,
How I enjoy this lovely view.

Not Your Average Fairy Tale

Cinderella had it made,
Her fairy tale will never fade.
A ball, a gown, her charming prince!
It's just enough to make you wince…

Snow White and her seven dwarfs,
Found true love in a man on a horse.
Woodlands and flowers everywhere!
It's just enough to curl your hair…

And then that Belle, had an actual beast,
Even she had the grandest feast.
Books and teacups all around!
But something isn't all quite sound…

You see, that's not a fairy tale to me.
It's my husband and bonus kids 1, 2, 3.
Happily gathered round the table,
Now that's a more realistic fable!

The Day You Chose Bruce

On one such glorious and magical day,
You came into the room - "Music!" you say!
Of all the records there are to choose,
You picked my very favorite, Bruce.

I don't think you quite understand what this means,
To have this picked over "The Blondie's" or Queen.
I know they're your favorites but you chose him instead.
Be still my heart, and get ahold of my head!

This day will go down in the books,
To have the others overlooked.
Bruce is Boss, and number one.
Soon you'll too sing Born to Run!

Stepmom Friends

Gather we do occasionally,
To preserve each other's sanity.
Don't ever underestimate the power,
Of multiple stepmoms at happy hour!

There's always laughter and maybe some tears,
As we discuss it all over beers.
The highs, the in-betweens, and lows,
Of blended family splendor and woes.

If you don't have any stepmom friends,
This is something I recommend.
Start by looking for a group that's local,
Or start one yourself by being vocal!

The bond that these women have together,
Is something that will last forever.
They understand right away,
The joy and pain you feel each day.

Go have a cosmo, or glass of wine,
It's ok to chat and dine…
You work too hard not to take this break,
Don't miss this free therapy at stake!

Deep

These words may not be deep you say,
But we don't need deep to get through the day.
The reality is that we need a laugh,
A glass of wine, and a bubble bath.

These poems are not for the poetry critics,
The stick in the muds or the cynics.
They are for normal stepmoms far and wide,
Maybe to help restore some pride.

Stand tall and know that you are strong,
Trust your instincts, but admit when you're wrong.
I wrote these poems to bring you a smile,
Whether you're in Rochester or across the Nile.

The truth is, we don't need "deep,"
And please don't judge us when we weep.
Just a little pick-me up will do,
When we're down and feeling blue.

These poems are important you see,
Not just for my sanity,
But for stepmom's all around,
Please enjoy this book you've found.

Damn it All to Hell!

This day is not quite going well,
Goddamn it all to fucking Hell.
The sadness inside, I try to keep,
But I'm certainly no Meryl Streep.

Dear family, please understand,
That just the gentle to touch of your hand,
Can put my day back on track,
Why is it attention that I lack?

This day is not going quite well,
Goddamn it all to fucking Hell.
I try to keep my thoughts at bay,
But here is what I need to say…

Dear family, please comprehend,
That I only want us to be friends.
I know someday all will be well,
But today I'm damning it all to Hell.

Dear Mother of Them

Does she think it so horrid?
Does she think it so vile?
For her children to have
More love and more smiles?

Dear mother of them,
Dear woman in pain,
We must work together,
Don't do this in vain.

The girls need us,
The girls need stability.
We need not be friends,
But we need civility.

Dear mother of them,
Dear woman in pain,
I extend this olive branch,
Peace be its name.

One of My Own

How strong this bond I feel with you,
Yet we share no eyes of blue.
Biology is not in our parts,
Yet love is felt deep in our hearts.

The bond is strong I cannot lie,
So I wonder what I'll feel inside?
When my own comes to be born,
How my heart will be adorned!

Fear thee not my darling girls,
A new baby will change our world.
But my fondness for you will never bend,
For you, too, I'll love right to the end.

Do it Right

If I could go back, I'd do it right.
But what is right?
Why do I want to make you happy?
My right was with him,
Your right was not.
Why is your happiness my concern?

If I could go back, I'd do it right.
But what is right?
Why do I want you to like me?
You forced him out,
I don't understand.
Why must I justify everything?

If I could go back, I'd do it right.
But what is right?
Why do I want you to stop lying?
Friends understand,
Enemies do not matter.
Why do I feel I need to protect myself?

If I could go back, I wouldn't change a thing.
I could feel what was right.
Why should I care what you think?
Love matters,
Your thoughts are none of my business.
Why can't I let this go?

Love

What About Team Love?

Team Him versus Team Her,
You picked sides and it really hurt.

Team Her versus Team Him,
Friendship is lost because you judged on a whim.

What about team right?
What about team it was time?
What about team that was broken?
What about team you're my friend and I want you to be happy?

What about team happy?
What about team it was painful?
What about team someone hurt someone?
What about team let's learn all the details before making a decision?

What about team LOVE?

The Holidays

You get the morning,
We'll have them for dinner.
Ok – it's a plan,
Sounds like a winner!

No, you take them in the evening,
We'll have them for breakfast.
Ok – it's a plan,
Let's put this to rest!

You changed my mind,
You want them for church,
Ok – it's a plan,
Whatever works…

This is the last time,
"I promise," you say!
Ok – it's a plan,
See you Sunday!

This doesn't quite work,
Your parents are coming?
Ok – it's a plan,
Thanks for nothing!!!

Some Time...

I Need Some Time

I need some time to recognize,
That I'm not your first in anyone's eyes.
I need some time all to myself,
To be sad you said "I do" to someone else.
I need a little time to mourn,
That our baby won't be your first born.
I need some time to be ok,
That she is in our lives to stay.

First and Last

She was your first,
But I am your last.
Whatever there was,
It's in the past.

Together you did things,
We'll do them too.
What brings me comfort,
Is my love for you.

Vows and babies,
You did that alright.
Your experience, however,
Brings me comfort at night.

She was your first,
But I am your last.
Our love is forever,
'Till our last breath is cast.

Pondering Life

I'd really like to take some time,
To do some crafts, enjoy some wine.
But now I have a second job,
All my free time has now been mobbed.

Who knew how great the expense would be,
For child support and groceries.
I do believe that each day is a gift,
But sometimes I feel that I need a lift.

What keeps me going is their smiles,
And dreams of walking down the aisle.
If I'm this busy now though, I'm a little scared,
What happens when another is in our care?

I'd really like to take some time,
To do some crafts, enjoy some wine.
If I work hard now I'm sure to see,
That the gifts life has will come to me.

Blessed

Your smile, our home,
Date nights alone.
Grandparents, trips,
favorite beer sips.
Walks, Saratoga,
Family yoga.
Minimal fights,
movie nights.
The old dog and cat,
Your array of hats.
Our garden in pots,
Our very small lot.
Jobs, Good health,
Moderate wealth.
Friends, Time together,
Sunny weather.
Your coffee, my tea,
Our family.

Why Do I Let You?

Why do I even let myself care?
A frown I allow you to let me wear.

Why do I even let myself think?
A nervous breakdown is on the brink.

Why do I even let myself fester?
When you've never given me a thoughtful gesture.

Open House

Open house can be a treat,
Halfway through the year your teacher I meet.
Feeling like I'm second class,
With all the parents walking past.

My face is not on the family wall,
Even though I'm involved in it all.
Never shall I be mad at you though,
I'm sure when you're older you will know.

Your teacher gave me a great big smile,
This made me feel better for a while.
In his eyes I could tell he knew,
How very much I care for you.

Go Back Two Spaces..

One Step Forward, Two Steps Back.

I keep coming back to this,
Wanting to forgive and move on.
Every time I get close,
You add another con.

Why are you so vindictive?
We try to be accommodating.
You made the shots,
Yet you're the one complaining.

I would really like for once,
That he let out his anger too.
Maybe I am the awful one,
At the same level as you.

Trying to remain positive,
Driving by your street on my way -
Wanting to scream and yell,
I let you ruin my day.

Spring

A time for renewal,
A time for rain and flowers.
A time to wash it all away.

A time for hope,
A time for soil and gardens.
A time to grow anew.

A time for awakening,
A time for more light and warmth.
A time to soften the spirit.

A time for rejoice,
A time for peace and song.
A time to lift the soul!

Mother's Day

Thoughts bittersweet encompass me.
I am proud to be a stepmom,
But society does not agree.

Just because I have not given birth,
My life is still dedicated to them,
We should celebrate our worth!

Will I be recognized on this day?
By my family and friends?
Will anyone go out of their way?

Happy Mother's Day to you,
Biological or not –
You are deserving for all you do!

I Want to Make You Human

In my thoughts you are not a person,
You are a source of frustration and pain.
I want to make you human,
To know you have blood in your veins.

In my thoughts you do not have a soul,
You are someone who acts like she is better.
I want to make you human,
I want to write you a letter.

In my thoughts you are not too, a woman,
You are a slightly less type of version.
I want to make you human,
I want to sit with you in person.

In my thoughts I envision you hating me,
You would not humor me a cup of coffee.
I want to make you human,
How can I if you will not let me?

Mothership

I am not the mother,
I am the mothership.
I pursue,
I execute,
I succeed.

I am not the mother,
I am the mothership.
I focus,
I plan,
I deliver.

I am not the mother,
I am the mothership.
I evaluate,
I organize,
I follow through.

Olive Branch

Here's my olive branch to you,
Will you extend one to me too?
I don't want my days to go this way,
Worried about what you do or say.

Here's my olive branch to you,
It's hard to have this point of view.
I want things to be easy and right,
Is this not a battle you fight?

Here's my olive branch to you,
I'm wondering what you're going to do.
A note I sent just yesterday,
Hoping for a response in some way.

Here's my olive branch to you,
I'm wondering if I'll get a clue.
Do I even want to talk?
Is it too late for me to walk?

Here's my olive branch to you,
I just want what's right for the little two.
Maybe you have some ideas to share,
They need to know how much we care.

Confusion

You made us wait,
We didn't fight.
We waited to tell,
We did it right.

A year went by,
Before they knew.
I was bursting inside,
But we did right by you.

You didn't wait,
Life isn't fair.
You call the shots,
You don't care.

Is he your friend,
Or more than that?
The kids don't know,
And those are the facts.

Confusion was to be
Avoided you said.
But that's what you created,
In everyone's head.

Heavy Heart

I know I carry a heavy heart,
I do my best to breathe and be smart.
But the man I love is hurting too,
His heart must be heavier than I ever knew.

If I miss them so, then how can he be,
So put together, unphased, and free?
I know not why this grief he hides,
I want to be his shoulder, should he cry.

Is it possible he does not mind?
That she withholds them and is unkind?
I don't understand how this can be easy,
Because my heavy heart eats at me.

That is the question

To Publish or Not to Publish

Should I share my thoughts?
My deepest fibers,
With the world unknown?

Should I share my comfort?
My understanding,
With the women who know?

Should I take the risk?
In hurting the children,
With speaking so freely?

Should I use a fake name?
To mask myself,
With hopes to spare them?

Should I express myself?
Openly or privately,
What is the answer?

Pet Dynamics

Your old dog, and my old cat,
Hate each other and that is that.

In my dreams before they met,
I knew them to be cuddly pets.

Milo and Otis ruined my thought,
Instead I count the times they've fought.

The hissing and barking is never ending,
Even animals must adjust to blending.

My Future In-Laws

Were we ever meant to meet?
To find this friendship so very sweet?
You mustn't have known that I would be –
Your life was progressing perfectly.

But here I am and here we are,
Family quickly from the start.
Oh, natural comfort makes me at ease.
Thank you for this refreshing breeze.

You raised the man who I adore,
I couldn't ask for very much more.
But more I received and I do confess –
To love his parents, how I am blessed!

Haiku

To mother, or not?
To step away or react?
This is a tough call.

Each day different.
Wanting more consistency.
Learning to accept.

Need to embrace change,
But stick to the schedule.
Balance is key.

This easily said.
But so hard to follow through.
Teamwork is a must.

Veggie Snafu

In cooking I've learned a trick or two,
Don't put their veggies in a stew.
Instead make soup and blend it up,
Then ladle it in to a fancy cup.

Apparently if veggies are unidentifiable,
It makes them 100% less vile!
I've tried this more than once or twice,
Don't be afraid to skip the rice!

Last night was a white winter vegetable soup,
With turnip, potatoes, and white radish too!
Cauliflower, and kohlrabi I kid you not –
They ate it up right on the spot!

So next time you're in a veggie snafu,
Don't work yourself up and make your face blue.
Just put those veggies in a seasoned broth,
And blend it to a creamy froth!

Shopping

Going shopping with the gals,
Going out like we're best pals –
Until they see something they "need,"
In an awkward spot I am – indeed.

I try to explain that I don't pay,
So they might understand this way –
But trying to explain I lose my stance,
And they give me that pleading glance.

I need some help on this one please,
Do I give in or make them cease?
Money is not an easy topic,
But how we react requires some logic.

In the Back Seat

In the back seat,
I do not drive.
I sit and watch,
I can only ride.

I've always driven,
My whole life.
I have no say,
With his ex-wife.

Out of control,
Not in charge.
Someone else drives,
But this is my car!

This chauffer,
I did not hire.
She's the driver,
And I want her fired.

This is my car,
I want it back,
That's my front seat,
This is out of whack.

I want to drive,
How dare you take that,
This is my life,
Give it back!

I can't take the bull,
I can't take the horns,
This is not the end,
You have been warned.

Moving

I love my little house in the city,
The yard is small but the flowers pretty.
I can come and go as I please,
Walking or biking with the greatest of ease.

Eventually I'll need to move,
Because the city does not have the best of schools.
But I love it here, and I want to stay,
I suppose it cannot be that way.

I am destined to boring suburban life,
Can't wait to be neighbors with the ex-wife!
I think the future kids will be ok,
If we stay living the city way.

I know that school is one of the best,
Throughout the entire state no less,
But what if we just try our hand,
at living on the city's land.

Haiku 2

Your dad is away,
A week in San Francisco.
I do not see you.

The house is quiet.
Your stuffed animals eye me
From your room corner.

The night is empty.
My "family" has vanished.
One more week I wait.

Michaele Lynne B...

Last Names

Will you keep his last name too?
That would be very like you.
Like a pop song on replay,
You're unfortunately here to stay.

Selfish, spiteful, and slow to move,
You'll keep it like a point to prove.
You're undeserving of such a name,
It sickens me that we'll have the same.

Teenage Years

Teenagers are a scary breed,
Trying to look cool, wanting to be free.

I'm slightly terrified, I won't lie,
Of the inevitable rollercoaster ride.

For you, I'll always be there though,
Through all the highs and through the lows.

I hope that I can always provide,
Good advice and be a guide.

I may be able to help you out,
If with your parents you yell and shout.

I can play the middle-man,
I'll help you any way I can.

I am scared, but I'll admit I'm more excited,
Hoping we'll be good friends united.

New Eyes

I need to try harder,
To see with new eyes.
To focus on me,
to look towards the prize.

I need to look past,
With eyes anew.
To see the beauty,
I need to be true.

Life is too short,
I need to set free
My soul and spirit,
Of all this debris.

I owe it to myself
To take care and cherish,
My time here on earth,
For we all one day perish.

Go Away

Can't I even get away?
Even on my one vaca…
Your voice is loud right through the phone,
Please can you just leave me alone!

We must cater to the time,
That you can speak to them on the line.
But when their dad tries to call,
You don't pay attention to your phone at all.

ABC's

Co-Parenting A-B-C's!

Goals: Anticipate,
Acclimate, and Affiliate!

Reality: Abominate,
Alienate, and Annihilate.

Goals: Benefitting,
Behooving, and Befitting!

Reality: Bitter,
Bothersome, and Boisterous.

Goals: Communicate,
Cooperate, and Collaborate!

Reality: Complicate,
Consternate, and Castigate.

Now I know my ABC's,
Next time won't you co-parent with me!

S.O.S.

Help

My spark is gone,
My energy wiped.
My heart is heavy,
My chest is tight.

My hope is lost,
My passion is drained.
My head is pounding,
My heart is in pain.

My view is grim,
My blood pressure is high.
My outlook is grey,
I let out a sigh.

Perspective

Shifting my focus to future me,
My future kids and family.

While I love my steps without a doubt,
I can't allow myself to feel so put-out.

I am thankful for the things we do,
But I'll get to do it all again too!

I want to do it all and more,
But I guess that's what perspective's for.

It's OK if I'm not completely involved,
With my own baby I'll be fully enthralled.

Here Goes Nothing...

To Publish

It looks like this is happening,
It looks like this is real.
I'm going to pursue this dream,
I'm still not sure how I feel.

I'm excited, but I'm scared,
I'm happy, but under the gun.
For once it's really happened,
It can never be undone.

How will it feel to actually see
My poems in a book?
I envision holding it in my hands,
I envision you taking a look.

Dear Oldest

Dear Sweet Oldest One,
How difficult this can be.
You love your father and mother,
I'm not sure how you see me.

I want you to know I'm trying,
I want you to know I care.
Sometimes I feel like crying,
Sometimes it's hard to bear.

I know someday we'll figure it out,
I know someday it will end.
I guess for now perhaps we'll pout,
Until we figure out our blend.

Dear Youngest

Dear Sweet Youngest One,
How easy this all seems.
We hit the ground with a run,
I'm not sure what this means.

I hope it always stays this way,
But I will be prepared -
Because it's possible that someday,
For us, the sky's not so fair.

But for now I'll sit back and smile,
As you lay and cuddle with me.
I hope it's like this for all while,
How close I feel to thee.

Our Own

I want to see the look on your face,
When our child comes to be.
I want to know that bond you feel,
I want that to include me.

How patiently I try to wait,
For the right time to be ours.
To make something so precious with you,
I count down the days and hours.

I hope he has your eyes of blue,
The dimples would be so cute too.
I just can't wait to meet him soon,
How lucky he will be.

Many new parents go in scared,
But I have peace inside.
I've watched your love your children so,
A father with such pride.

About the Author:

Michaele-Lynne Jacot was born in Saratoga Springs, NY, where she grew up with her parents and younger brother until she graduated from Saratoga Springs High School in 2005. Not very athletic, she played the French horn in band from 5th grade until senior year (and still does!). She enjoyed art and music classes, and spending time with one or two best friends.

From 2005-2009 she lived in Potsdam, NY while she attended Clarkson University for her Bachelors of Science in Psychology. Late in her career at Clarkson, Miss Jacot decided that she wanted to study Organizational Psychology and Group Dynamics. She applied to the Industrial/Organizational Psychology Master's program at West Chester University of Pennsylvania and studied there from 2009-2011.

Upon graduation she found herself reconnected with a friend who had recently become single - as had she. She hesitantly accepted a date to a concert in Philadelphia, where she lived at the time, knowing that she could easily fall for him – yet the situation was more than complicated. After one year of long distance she moved back home to Saratoga Springs where she worked for about a year before deciding that she and her boyfriend were ready to live together in Rochester, NY where he resided with his two young daughters. The first couple years of their relationship was very strained due to outside factors and influences beyond their control (if you've ever dated a man with children from a previous relationship you understand!).

Today Miss Jacot and her boyfriend of four years live in Rochester, NY where she works as a Human Resources professional. They live with his two daughters (7 and 9) with whom he has split custody and hope to be married in the not so distant future.

Miss Jacot enjoys arts and crafts, traveling, sampling different teas, dining out, craft beer, yoga, Zumba, golf, and watching hockey. Oh, and Stepmom gatherings!!

www.ingramcontent.com/pod-product-compliance
Lightning Source LLC
Chambersburg PA
CBHW042339150426
43195CB00006B/111